pity party

A COLLECTION OF POEMS BY KYLER O'NEAL

Pity Party

Designed by: Mitch Green at Rad Press Publishing

YOU'RE INVITED TO A PARTY!

This book is a collection of pieces I've written throughout the course of my life during some of the most difficult times where I felt emotionally low. I gathered them all together and would like to share them with you. It may sound odd but sometimes knowing that someone else is out there suffering too can help ease the sting of life's burdens. You somehow don't feel as inadequate or alone as circumstances may sway you to believe. Most of these poems cover not-so-joyous topics. I hope that you are able to connect with the content and/or even gain some perspective from it. So without further ado, let's have a pity party.

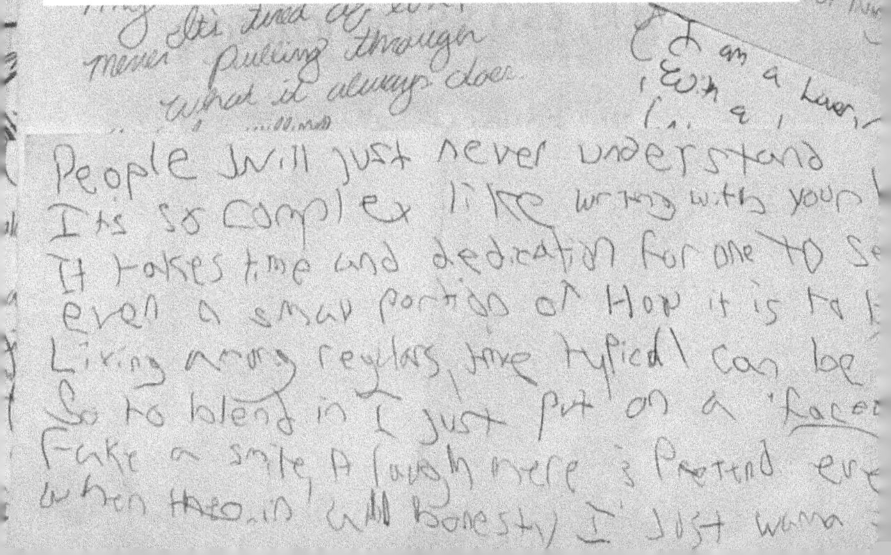

Losers
ONLY!

CONTENTS

PART III

DEAR GOD,

I hate this planet,
I don't fit in.
I always lose,
And have yet to win.
I have bad luck
With people I like,
And get treated badly
From left to right.
I hate my skin,
I hate my hair.
When you created my race
Did you even care?
No one likes us
Not even each other.
And this makes me skeptical
Of becoming a mother.
Each day I wish
That I would die,
And be free to roam
Up in the sky.
I should be thankful
But I hate my life.
I'm always done wrong,
Hardly ever right.
I don't know why,
You put me here!
What was the point?!
It's so unclear!
Seems all I do

Is please them all.
Then they all leave
Me when I call.
I hate this planet
And I want out.
And when I see you,
There's a lot we'll talk about.

written in Los Angeles

... and at some point, all the hurt kept inside starts to bleed out.

PART I

DAY I IN THE WORLD: MIDWESTERN STATE OF MIND PT. I

Today's my first day in the world.
I'm lookin' forward to livin'.
Can't wait to make new friends,
Be happy, free, & simply livin'.
I can't wait to trust,
Trust people I once never knew,
And look at them as my new siblings.
And love them despite all we go through.
Of course my feelings they'll return,
Cause the world looks like a beautiful place.
Where no one wants to harm each other,
Or see an unhappy face.
I look forward to being encouraged
As I've been so at home.
To be comforted in times of stress,
And to never be left alone.
Today is my first day in the world,
And I'm so anxious to start.
Cause if things are as great as they are back home,
Then happiness & I will never part.

written in Cincinnati

WHAT CAN YOU TELL ME

What do you tell a person who's never had someone
To officially call their own?
Whose confidence is so strong
'til they realize they're alone.
What explanation is there
For a sad case such as this?
Is it their looks? Their personality?
Or their uniqueness that everyone seems to miss?
When I gaze into the mirror
One thing remains clear to me.
That I am a great catch like no other.
But this no one seems to see.
I've never been praised in that way before
Nor do I know how it feels
To be loved & cherished for who I am
To experience a romance so real.
Will someone please tell me what's wrong with me?
Why can't I get a decent date?
Why whenever I make an effort I get turned down
Or treated like 2nd rate?
I know I have a lot to offer
So much to make someone's life.
But no one will give me the chance
No one wants me in their life.
I wish I was a video girl
Someone everyone was attracted to
Whose beauty is almost never ignored.
Who's endlessly praised and valued.
Her man can look at her and be so proud

To have somethin' special everyone doesn't.
To have someone that'll make others jealous
Away from her side he'd wish he wasn't.
Yeah video girls are everywhere
Not just on the TV
Some live around the corner, or are in the club.
Some... but not me.
I'm no drop-dead gorgeous dime piece
Hell I really don't know my worth.
All I know is that I'm a great catch,
And that I've been that from birth.

written in Cincinnati

...but a smile can only hide so much.

DAY I IN THE WORLD... PT.2

Today was my first day in the world,
So disappointing, so wrong.
I do not understand this place
And how negativity is so strong.
Why can't I travel from point A to point B
Without there being tension in the air?
What is everyone so mad about?
Why doesn't anyone care?
Care for others how I care for my brothers,
Or how my mother cares for me?
Why can't we all be loving & friendly
And like one big happy family?
Why is a cold shoulder so acceptable,
And a daily factor of life?
Why is pessimism key?
To always expect the worst in life?
This place is nothing like home,
Where we actually love each other & care.
This place is more like a hell.
Full of difficulty & despair.
Why do people tease me for who I am?
Back home I was loved.
What's so hard about accepting others?
Why can't we all be loved?
I do not understand this world.
And why skin tone matters.
Or why people will push others down,
To climb ahead on the ladder.
How can someone not know?

Know how to love?
But know hate in its place,
Killing and stealing and all of the above.
Why is heartbreak so common in this place?
As opposed to love unconditionally.
Why does happiness seem like a fairytale?
A myth that can never be?
Today was my first day in the world.
And I never wanna go back.
This place was not what I expected,
This wasn't my natural habitat.

written in Cincinnati

NORMAL = PERFECT (PRELUDE)

People will just never understand.
It's so complex like writing with my left hand.
It takes time & understanding for one to see,
A glimpse of what it's like to be a loser like me.
Living among all these regular people gets hard,
So I go out of my way to blend and put on a façade.
Fake an image, put on a smile, as if all is okay.
When in all honesty, I just want to take my life away.

written in New York

THEY GET YOU

You don't have to try,
You're immediately understood.
No one dismisses your presence
Or expects you to be up to no good.
If you act wild and crazy
It's totally fine.
No one will get too upset or judge
Especially not your own kind.
Your aesthetic appeal
We all know, love and embrace.
It's become the nation's barometer
For most beauty standards in place.
Be it corporate or social America
You are the norm.
The behavioral standard deemed ideal
No questions asked, no reform.
From your hairstyles, lifestyle and fashion trends,
To the way you talk
Media praises your existence.
You've got the pedestal on lock.
People want you in their circle.
I watch 'em gravitate to you
For your "approachableness" or their subconscious desire
For validation from your elite crew.
What I envy most though is how you can get
Just about any guy
Of any race, any nationality
Your chances are far greater than mine.
Whether one knows your story or not

You'll always be "gotten."
Whether you want to know it or not
You're kinda spoiled rotten.
Not dismissing your problems at all
I just *want* you to see,
How you win by default on many social platforms,
Of this unfair society.

written in Los Angeles

UNTITLED

After a certain period of time,
It gets hard to hold back the tears.
To hide the pain, the disappointments,
Frustrations, anger and the fears.
It seems like on a daily basis,
I find myself always wearing a mask.
Playing my role and staying in my lane,
Answering correctly should anyone ask.
Can't help but notice what everyone else has.
Can't help but think "why can't that be me?"
But then I come to my senses and remember,
How much I don't fit in with this society.
Encountering hate from every angle,
Just for being myself in the now
I've come not to love myself so much,
And really don't know how.
How can an outcast truly love themselves
When all they know is hate?
How can you expect me to want to live
When my life has been far from great?
I'm misunderstood, I don't belong,
And I probably will never be
The opposite: happy in this world,
And accepted by society.
It's easy to blow off social acceptance,
When you're essentially part of the norm.
But when you're an outcast like myself,
Acceptance is the end goal,
That helps you push through life's storms.

written in Cincinnati

NORMAL = PERFECT

To be normal is to be perfect,
Believe it or not.
'Cause it's never a big deal
When you've got what everyone's got.
Even abnormalities aren't as "abnormal"
As they're perceived to be.
Unless your abnormality is a minority
Among many in its extreme.
"You've got so much to live for!"
Is what people like to say.
Not realizing how *living* can seem more painful,
Than throwing your life away.
When you're a fish in a big pond of so many,
More alike than they realize,
You start to question your self-worth,
The desolation gets harder to disguise.
So what is there to live for
When you're constantly suffering by the hour?
Longing for love and acceptance
But simultaneously losing all willpower.
With no one to call who'll understand
Or make you feel okay,

An endless fear of more rejection,
Extreme caution by the day.
Why live when chances are
There appears to be no reason to?
Think long and hard about these words
Then tell me, what you would do?

written in Cincinnati

MEDIA SCARES ME

"Go see a movie?"
No thanks, not me.
I'm tired of watching "winners"
Who don't look like me.
I'm tired of watching stories
That to my life don't relate.
That make me question my value
Or sometimes heighten my self-hate.
A hot new celebrity? No thanks.
I'd rather spare my mind.
Chances are they're probably racist
Or don't even associate with my kind.
I'm tired of all this media
Portraying "what beauty is."
I'm tired of the subconscious brainwashing
Skewed by marketing biases.
I'm over falling prey,
To someone else's agenda.
I'm tired of seeing realities
Created by a bunch of pretenders.
For years these mediums showed me
That I barely exist in their world.
And that my darker skin and hair texture
Somehow makes me less of a desirable girl.
I'd rather not consume anymore
I'll leave it to you guys.
'Cause my brain's over the mental abuse
That my hypersensitivity has come to realize.

written in Los Angeles

IN MY COMFORT ZONE

... I am confident all alone.
No worries about what others think.
No paranoia of negative energy
Just me, my bed & thoughts.
That's really all I need.
And every so often for entertainment,
I'll have some company.
Let them use me for my body
In exchange for their attention.
Then let them leave my life,
Without warning or mention.

written in New York

CANCERIAN PARANOIA

Throughout my life I've seen many things
Words cannot express.
From smiles, laughter, good times, & joy,
To pain, betrayal, ruin & unrest.
Friends who appear to be one way,
But later on let you down.
People who claim they'll be there for you,
But in the end are nowhere to be found.
Though my life has only just begun,
I've learned so much so soon.
Not to trust anyone despite how they seem,
And to never let an association bloom.
Bloom into something beyond polite conversation,
Or turn into something more.
Like an actual friendship or love, what everyone wants.
A concept us lonely folk adore.
Nah, I've been that route plenty of times.
And nobody ever came through.
These wounds I have, I'm used to them
And I'll trust no one - nope, not even you.

written in Cincinnati

DEAR LIFE...

Dear Life,
You've got some balls,
First you fuck me over,
Then you fuck me raw.
No matter how high
I put up my guard
You always find some way,
To tear me apart.
I'm tired of this battle,
I wanna throw in the towel.
I want freedom from this misery
And I need it right now!
Day by day,
I get weaker and weaker
With nothing to look forward to,
But a future that seems bleaker.

written in New York

A MESSAGE TO DISNEY

You had an influence. You left your mark.
You gave me hope & fear, all in one spark.
And now it's time, to give me some answers,
Hear the random thoughts, of this zodiac Cancer.

All those fairytales, I grew up watchin'
Created expectations, & got me mentally rotten.
I'm tryna make, sense of it all
And all I really want, is you to help me solve.
Yeah, I was just a child, but now I'm grown
So I wanna know, about what wasn't shown:

That fair-white, Snow girl, was she really happy?
Or was she way too fly, to settle with one Papi?
Did she ever get sick, of Prince Proper Clean-Cut?
Did she ever crave, someone Huntsman tough?

That Beauty girl, boo'd up with The Beast
Was she sexually happy? Was he too rough in the sheets?

That one blonde-haired girl, Known for always sleepin'
Was her man loyal? Or while she slept he'd be creepin'?
Was she ever interested in pursuing girls?
It was sixteen whole years 'til she saw a boy in the world.

That other blue-eyed girl, who could fit the shoe.
Was she satisfied, marrying a snob with no clue
To what a struggle was, or poor living conditions,
Where no one cares, or even pays you attention?
Could she really relate, to someone so wealthy
From a different class with status so healthy?
And if that weren't the case, would you ever say
That she was a gold-digger, who came from rags just to slay?

And last but not least, my main question of all.
Please tell me why, every "princess" I saw
Who always won The Guy, never looked like me,
'Til I was a teenager passed 2003?
Like "If you're brown, then you ain't happenin'
That is unless you look like Jazmin."
Did you ever think, that I existed too?
Or was I not worthy enough to your marketing crew?
See the sad part is, your films were watched by all.
Not just by the race, most of your characters were.

You're one of the reasons, I still have hope
But also a reason, I'm looked at as a "nope."
It even throws me off, when I still see
All your princess ads that still exclude Tianee.
Like it or not, your content conditions
You entertained us yes, but really failed to mention
How life's more complex, beyond the 60 minutes
That other shade tones exist, other bodies worth attention.
If I ever have kids, I'll simply let them watch
Your animal movies only 'cause I'll be damned if I botch
Their vulnerable minds, and innocent perceptions
All for the sake, of your prioritized mentions.
Please keep in mind, this is not a diss.
I just had to ask. Make it, make sense.
Feel free to respond, won't be surprised if you don't.
I'm just an average Jill, possess millions I don't.
And to the readers of this, who think I'm just fussin
These are just my thoughts, not for debate or discussion.

written in Los Angeles

NYC STATE OF MIND

Do you know what it's like to be alone?
Even in a city with millions of people crammed in one zone?
To crawl into a large bed & only be touched by linen & pillows?
To only be kissed by the open window's billows?
In your most miserable moments to have no one to hold your head,
To the point where you bury your tearful face into a wall instead?
When the only person you can communicate with is yourself & a bunch of nonliving things,
And you're trying your hardest to figure out what all of this means?
To look in the mirror and, each time, fall prey to your own thoughts,
Find new insecurities to justify this lonesomeness that you've got.
To fear the thing you desire most & its ability to break you,
Yet crave it so badly that just about anything will do.
To gaze upon strangers in total desperation,
For eye contact, interest, engagement, some kind of connection,
Yet get almost nothing in return but disregarded each time,
To the point that it starts to get to you and screws with your mind.
To see yourself one way, but get treated another,
And to be forced to accept it, one way or the other.
To look at a passing truck each time & wonder,
If this will be the day you decide to go under.
This is my reality each & everyday,
And each effort to change it, usually results in more disarray.
But if you were to ask, I'd say "everything's okay."
Although, I'm slowly losing myself, each and every day.

written in New York

ALONE ON CHRISTMAS

Another holiday season
is here once again.
No family around to celebrate,
nor ones I call "friend."
As I'm surrounded by all this holiday cheer,
Via the masses,
I ponder what to do with myself
Until this time passes.
Should I walk around the area
And stroll aimlessly?
Or go interact with the workers
At 7-Eleven or Coffee Bean?
I've already checked my dating apps
At least twenty times.
Once more won't hurt I guess,
I might land a match so sublime.
My neighbors are having a party.
I can hear them loud and clear.
Maybe I'll drop by and try my best
Not to be awkward or queer.
'Tis a beautiful, yet awkward time
where people question your activity.
Not expecting to hear at all
That you've spent it alone... pathetically.
Being alone is nothing new for me
This is just another day.
But the thought keeps ricocheting in my mind:
How no one should be alone on Christmas Day.

written in Los Angeles

WHY MISERY LOVES COMPANY

She needs to know she'll be okay
She needs to look forward to a brighter day.
She needs to know she's not alone
That she's not the only one broken and wronged.
She needs a shoulder to cry and relate to
To help ease the pain of what she goes through.
She needs someone to help her cope
But most importantly, to help her not give up hope.
You think she's annoying but all she wants
Is not another back turned from her, but instead someone's front.

written in Los Angeles

PART II

THE GAME OF LOVE

Here's a game for us to play,
When there's nothin' left to do.
But before we rush right into things like everyone else
Let us first examine the rules.
To play this game you need one team
Traditionally made up of two.
Now however many other players get involved
Well that decision is up to you.
You should know before getting started,
This ain't no Tic-Tac-Toe.
If you play this game you're risking your life
So if you're scared I suggest you go.
So without further ado let's begin
Everyone put on your gloves.
'Cause things can get really messy,
When you're playing the game of love.

Now this game usually starts
With a guy & a girl.
Should you choose otherwise
Then you may be hated by the world.
The two must like each other,
& build a bond like no other.
Then try not to share this bond

That is so strong with another.
Others may try to join your team
For selfish motives only.
But being strong & well disciplined
Will help you avoid this only.
This game can get very challenging.
Your body may even turn on you.
It may steer you in the wrong direction,
'Causing you to do things, in hindsight you don't wanna do.
Let's say that you see someone
Who you're physically attracted to.
You're feelin' them a lot,
But you love your partner too.
An extra man, or woman, in this game
Most likely won't benefit you at all.
Instead of getting you to the next level
It may bring you to a fall.
No one said this game would be easy
That's why you should think before getting involved
'Cause although there's two in the relationship
You must unite as one for the problems to be solved.
It's only as difficult as you make it.
This team is a major commitment.
If you know within that you can't do it
Then we suggest you don't fool around with it.
How the game is won remains unknown
But it doesn't all end with a ring.
For a team that successfully makes it to the finish line
Is a game that remains to be seen.

written in Cincinnati

THIS GUY...

So there's this guy I'm getting to know,
Who makes me feel good, & makes me glow.
He gives me no reason to feel insecure,
And reassures me that his feelings are sure.
Sometimes idk what to think about my new beau.
Cause sometimes it's as if he's too good to be true.
Every guy from my past always up and disappeared,
But it's been a couple months and this guy is still here.
This guy makes me feel like I'm okay.
Like there's nothing wrong with me & I should feel no other way.
This guy gives me hope, something I've learned to fear,
Cause whenever I get hopeful about someone, they tend to disappear.
I like this guy so much, I've let my guard down
When deep down I know he may not always be around.
Still I appreciate his kindness and for giving me new hope.
For making me feel worth something, worth more than dope.
This guy's pretty cute too, with really nice eyes.
His good looks kind of intimidate me, more than he may realize.
I wonder if I'd be enough, to satisfy his desires
His physical & emotional needs, wants, & whatever else is dire.
Only time will tell if he was worth picking up a paper & pen.
Brief or lasting, only the future knows & I won't know 'til then.
But for now he's what makes me happy, what brings me good joy.
And I appreciate the man he is, & how he's not some little boy.
My wrist is starting to hurt & I'm running out of lines that rhyme.
So I guess I'll quit babbling on, about this really cool Guy.

written in New York

PLEASE STAY

I know that tone & recognize those eyes.
It's that fade I know too well that brings me to cries.
When the honeymoon high falls,
And you answer less when I call.
Your heart seems less fonder
And your brain begins to wander.
Your tone goes from inviting to rough.
And you make it apparent that I'm not enough.
Yet still I latch on, hurt & stressed
'Cause to me you're all I want to caress.
I was convinced you wouldn't do this too,
Yet I already see what I'm about to go through.

Around you my arms wrap tight,
My voice frail & fright.
Like a child I plead & beg to you,
Not to do what you once said you wouldn't do.
As pitiful as I may seem
I still wish this were all a dream.

Say what you want & I will supply
I'll buy the hair, change my skin, even the color of my eyes.

Whatever you want I'll get done
Whoever you want I'll become
Whatever it takes to make you see,
Here with me is where you should be.
I'm begging you, please don't walk away.
I'll do anything... just... please... stay.

written in New York

OPEN RELATIONSHIP = LET'S PRETEND

Let's pretend we're in a relationship
Though we both know
We're just settling for each other
'Til we find a more desirable foe.
We'll slap a label on this rapport
For the sake of peace of mind
Rather than acknowledge it for what it really is
Something convenient to help pass time.
We'll pretend we're in love and stuff
And invite others in our world
Subconsciously auditioning other candidates
'Til we find a more ideal guy or girl.
And once that happens,
Then all bets are off.
This "relationship" we claim we're in
Will show its true colors off.
But in the meantime we've got each other,
So neither of us have to be alone,
But my promiscuous choices are not up for discussion
And no conflicts of interest should ever be shown.

written in Los Angeles

I'LL SETTLE

For you, I'll settle
for any treatment you give.
Bite my tongue, do anything you want,
Any fuck up I'll forgive.
What can I say? I'm desperate.
Plus you're all I've ever wanted.
A guy like you is a dream come true
I'm flattered and slightly daunted.
Usually guys like you
Don't even look my way.
So even if it's just your minimal interest
I'll do whatever for you to stay.
Use my body, take advantage
I consent to whatever you please
In exchange for this validation
Of the loser that lives within me.

written in Los Angeles

WHEN IT'S NOT YOU PT.I

It's easy to disregard
How you make someone feel.
It's effortless to prance around
And always be real.
It comes as second nature
To be and stay true to you,
Especially when no consequences
Are there to await you.
Go anywhere at anytime
And do as you please.
Use a body, break a heart
Waste someone's time, move on with ease.
No need to think twice,
Your options are in endless supply,
It's all a matter of who meets your criteria
That determines the treatment you apply.
Replace one after the other,
With no notice at any given time.
'Cause you're the "catch" everyone wants,
To be around or have in their life.
Spoiled by life's shallow standards,
It's likely you'll never see
How significantly good you have it
Or how worse off you could be.
No need to make efforts,
When they're almost all made for you.
No need to consider the pain you cause others,
Especially when it's not you.

written in Los Angeles

NOTHING TO GIVE

I have nothing to offer nothing to give
For you I cannot be.
All of the things that you look for, the norm,
The standard of your society.
I don't have the looks, or ability to make your peers envious
In my life this gift does not apply.
I can't give you the lovin' you prefer.
I cannot & probably won't ever qualify.
All that I have to give
Is what seems valuable to me
And that is my all in all love,
Affection, loyalty & security.
However, this does not reach your standards,
And that you have made clear.
I've learned there could never be an us
No matter how clear in my mind the vision appears.
In my mind I have so much to offer to you,
I'd be the home you'd love to live.
But in reality what I am you don't want
And in reality I have nothing to give.

written in Cincinnati

THEN CAME YOU...

I never understood,
Why people didn't like me
Or how just being myself
Could motivate someone to dislike me.
I never understood,
Why I was never called by name.
But instead called insults
As if I were the one to blame.
Take the blame for what?
I was just bein' me.
Guess that, that wasn't good enough but
Who else was I supposed to be?
I never fit in with my peers
They've always pushed me away.
Or stabbed me in the back
For someone else's gain.
I was very lonely back then,
Then you came along.
You made me feel like somebody,
As if I could do no wrong.
You made me feel valuable.
Like a jewel bought from Tiffany's.
Like a winning lotto ticket.
As if I were perfect with no flaws of any.
I finally discovered confidence.
How to not bother or care
About what anyone had to say about me.
How to purposely be unaware.
Your love showed me that I was okay

That I didn't need to change.
I wish we would've lasted forever
But things were rearranged.
It started to throw me off
When you began to barely notice me.
When you were out & I was in
Wanting to be wherever you would be.
Then you left for good with no warning
As if you were some coward.
Left me alone in a bed
Caressing pillows by the hour.
Neglected all over again.
Didn't see it coming from you.
All the pain I thought had disappeared
Had instantly returned... and with interest too.

written in Cincinnati

WTF...

Why claim you want one thing,
Then show me another?
Why hold & console me,
Then say you don't want to be smothered?
Why touch me lovingly
& kiss me with passion
And act as if it'll have no impact
on my feelings or rational?
Why even build a rapport,
Past the sexual part?
Why say "no strings" at first,
Then sew actively towards my heart?
You come, you cum, you go was the agreement.
With no doubts, questions or murmurs.
But all the cuddles, "I miss yous" & inviting me out
Had me convinced that you wanted us to go further.
You're accountable for your words yes,
But your actions even more!
So don't try to act as if
You didn't lead me to expect more.
You built me up then broke me down
In a worst possible way.
And what sucks most about all this
Is how you expect me to just be okay.

written in New York

UNTITLED

I wish that you could see things
The way that I do.
If only you could understand
My overlooked point of view.

When you're afraid to speak your mind
'Cause of how it'll make you look
It gets difficult to express your thoughts
& be an open-book.

I wish you'd step outside your comfort zone
& into my world.
I wish you'd crave me like how guys
Crave that celebrity-girl.

I wish you'd realize how difficult
It gets for me to please you.
And how living up to your standards
Is not an easy thing to do.

I wish you'd see me for who I am,
One heck of a catch
And that if given the chance I'd show you
How this could be the perfect match.

Just as I accept your flaws,
I wish for me you'd do the same
Instead of making me feel obligated
To just bring glory to your name.

I wish you'd think as highly of me,
The way that I do you.
Although you're not perfect, there's no one else
I'd rather call beau.

You are my world, my everything,
No possession's worth more than you.
But these feelings you do not reciprocate,
I seem worthless to you.

You'd much rather have what everyone wants.
Ideals created by media and magazines
But what you fail to realize is the fact
That nothing is ever as good as it seems.

For every plus, there is a minus.
Every person has a flaw.
Whether internal or externally the reality is,
No one can have it all.

One day you'll regret screwin' this up,
And realize how naïve you are
For missing out on one heck of a person,
Better than any "perfect girl" or pricy car.

Gave you a chance 'cause you were cute,
And now I've fallen so deep
Even lowered my standards & altered myself
To try & be who you want me to be.

Like Hera & Zeus, I've realized
That this "relationship" will never work.
Even though this truth is hard to embrace
And my mind it will continually irk.

Whatever shall I do? Keep loving you
In hopes that you'll come around?
That you'll finally appreciate this rare stone you have
That no one has ever found?

At this point I think I'll throw in the towel,
Who knows if that day will ever come.
Wasting more of my time waiting on you
Would only make both of us dumb.

written in Cincinnati

THE "I'M POLY!" TRANSLATION

"Commit-whaaat?! I'm greedy
I can't commit to just one.
That's more discipline than I care to have.
I just want endless fun.
Yeah, you're cool, but you're not really enough
To satisfy my crave.
You're worth keeping around for now
But not worth the exclusive pay."

written in Los Angeles

A BIG DICK = A BIG DICK

Great sex is most likely guaranteed
Then almost always followed by
Ignored calls, or no communication at all,
Or recurring delayed replies.
"NSA" disclaimers are usually made upfront
To avoid any liability for
The power they posses in their pants
And it's addicting ability to shake one's core.
Oh how lucky is the one
Worthy, in their eyes, of their commitment.
Oh how unlucky are the rest of us,
Whom fall prey to their pleasure, followed by resentment.

written in Los Angeles

I WISH I LIKED GIRLS!

I wish I liked girls.
There's clearly no shortage of supply.
And so many want what I want:
Love and loyalty 'til we die.
I can't help but think
How smoother dating would be,
Without worrying about the attention deficit disorder
Of my mate's eyes, mind or body.

written in Los Angeles

MY "I'M POLY" REACTION

You say you're Poly,
That commitment is a construct,
And we shouldn't suppress our animalistic design.
I say that's total bullshit
And that you're completely out of your mind.
The problem with the world today
Is we want everything fast and easy,
We don't want to wait or be disciplined
And we want to endlessly satisfy our greed.
The reality is when you do meet *that person,*
Your loyalty will come natural.
Exclusivity won't seem like a chore at all
Nor like something that is "unnatural."
Nothing ever comes easy, that's for sure.
We all know this to be true.
But when you do come across that one person
You'll be surprised by all you'll do.
So quit using people for the sake of convenience
And sugar coating it with that label
And acting as if no harm is being done
'Cause you and I both know that's one big fable.

written in Los Angeles

sometimes you crave affection so much, you'll take it in any form...

FAKE LOVE...

Kiss me with passion
Hold me tight.
Share intimate moments
All through the night.
Then the next day
Leave me be.
Live your life
And be free.
Fight with me sometimes,
As if it's real.
Pretend you care
'Til you're over the thrill.
Tell me I'm pretty,
Make me feel worth it.
Contradict my reality
Simply & cause I deserve it.
Don't want us seen?
Okay, that's fine.
Behind closed doors only,
Is where you'll be mine.
Say you love me,
Though we both know,
You don't mean those words
& your actions prove it so.
True, mom always told me,
Never settle for less
But I don't have that luxury
Of only attracting the best.
So I'll let you use me,
Simply in exchange

For the illusion & fantasy
Of me being worth claim.
You have your freedom,
To see & do,
Whatever or whomever
And I'll play it cool.
Pathetic as it seems
Being alone is no fun.
Especially when it's been the case
For most of my life-run.
So I'll keep pretending
Like you're sent from above
For as long as you keep giving me,
Your fake love.

written in New York

DENIAL

I'll rarely look in your direction,
I won't lose myself in your perfection.
I won't chase nor hope for your attention
Though my mind craves & sees it as pension.
I refuse to look like another groupie-hoe.
Can't let my ego suffer another blow.
Just keep my distance, and admire from a far
And never let you know how perfect to me you are.

written in Los Angeles

DEAR MIND

Give me a break will ya?
Just chill the heck out!
The last thing I need in life,
Is another crush to obsess about!
I was getting along just fine,
'Til you decided to take over,
With these unrealistic fantasies,
Dreams and hopes of the sober.
Haven't we endured enough?
Or must I suffer more?
Shall I tame you with more distractions,
Or use substances to settle the score?
At this point I'll do whatever it takes,
To prolong an emotional vacation.
Just stay in your peaceful state a little longer,
And let my heart regain formation.

written in Los Angeles

UNPROTECTED: HE LIKES ME

"This one will be different"
I say in my mind, to ease the uncertainty.
"He'll stick around, and won't abandon me,"
As I let him enter inside me.
"I've craved this connection for so long"
I coaxingly think to myself,
As I release all suppressed desire and energy
And put at risk my health.
His features, strength, size and girth
Are all I could ever want.
I look into his eyes and want to submit
And love him, not disappoint.
Blinded by emotion and my state of arousal
I completely disregard
How this could just be a convenient hookup for him,
And that this "connection" is just a facade.
Desperate to feel some kind of love
I accept it in any form
And hope that this one won't have consequences,
That this one will be different from my norm.

written in New York

NOTE TO SELFIE...

It's not right,
And you probably won't even be okay.
So sleep with as many of them as needed,
To help numb the pain away.
This numbness may not last long.
But it'll make a great distraction,
'Til you're ready to take that risk again
& snap back into action.
Until then, take all the time needed
'Til you're over that douche,
& all the others before him who came
& brutally damaged you.
Being nice & delicate has only gotten you
A broken heart & a fist full of tears,
Endless disappointments, shattered hopes,
A damaged mind, heart & soul that'll last years.
So next time be smarter! Don't fall so quick!
Put your guard up even higher!
And if he's really the one for you
He won't run away from your fire.

written in Los Angeles

violent, because I’m done being nice.

THE FIRE IN ME

The fire in me can't take any more.
The fire in me wants to settle the score.
Set the record straight for what they've all done,
In the past, present and all those to come.
The fire in me says, "keep calm no more"
If he treats you badly knock his ego to the floor.
Be it mentally or physically, be ready to make 'em pay.
For all this damage done that will never go away.
Wanna fuck me over? You'd better think twice.
'Cause that once merciful me is no longer quite as nice.

written in Los Angeles

ENDLESSLY

VIOLATED

IN

LIFE

SATAN'S TEARS (SONG)

Anyone ask you how you feel?
Did anyone notice that you're real?
Anyone say that you are loved?
Or that you're the one they're dreaming of?
... no...
You carry the weight of the world all in your head.
... and no-...
-one cares to ask or even notices that you're standing there.

Trying your hardest to fit in,
Seems like with that you never win.
Want them to see how great you are,
But with that you never get too far.
... and oh...
You carry all this disappointment deep inside
... and oh...
They all come and go then leave you there just to be alone and cry.

Satan's tears...
Satan's tears...
They don't get you, they don't appreciate you,
You feel insignificant.
Satan's tears...
Satan's tears...

Tried to see a brighter day,
Evil's not born it's made.
Gotta make some sense of this loneliness inside.
Once loving now bitter and jaded.
So qualified yet so underrated.
Tell me how will you survive?

Now you're angry at the world,
Judgment clouded by your pain
Want everyone to hurt like you
Lost in your sadness and your shame
... and no-...
one even notices you're slowly dying deep inside.
... and it seems like no one...
Could even give a damn as to whether or not you're dead or still alive.
... you're dead or still alive.

Satan's tears...
Satan's tears...
If I could touch you,
I'd wipe your tears and show you that you are not alone.
Satan's tears...
Satan's tears...
Satan's tears...
Satan's tears...

You're worthy too
Just see this through
I'm here for you
... you are not alone.

IT'S YOUR TURN

These next two pages are yours. Do as you please with them. Write a poem or a song, a letter, draw a picture, express random thoughts... whatever comes to your mind. Simply grab a writing utensil and go to town. If nothing comes to you at this given moment, simply leave the pages blank.
They'll be waiting for you when the time comes.

PART III

THE COMMON DENOMINATOR (MONOLOGUE)

I'll admit, I have low self-esteem... for many reasons. One especially is because I've seen & experienced what the power of attraction can do & it's ability to, sometimes irrationally, lock someone's interest in another whom they're really attracted to. Yet just about every guy I show interest in flees either before or not long after meeting me. All different kinds of guys, different backgrounds, one common denominator... me.

I've seen a girl attract multiple guys in the same night & make-out with just about all of them (unapologetically & blatantly) & still attract more guys in addition to the ones she attracted prior. I've seen it many times yet have never experienced what it must feel like to be That Girl.

I've had guys I've gone on dates with blatantly check-out, interact with & sometimes even flirt with or hit on another girl who caught their eye while we were together. All different kinds of guys, different backgrounds, one common denominator... me.

So you see, when I hear those BS sayings like "beauty's only skin deep" or that "it's what's on the inside that counts," I can't help but replay in my mind the countless times I've watched beauty prevail over "what's inside." 'Cause my golden personality has yet to score me a win in the dating game.

REALITY CHECK

Don't make eye contact.
Try not to stare.
Chances are, he's not interested.
Why? 'Cause you don't even compare,
To the type of girl he probably goes for
That "type"that always wins.
You're not even close to that kind of beauty
So why even try to pretend?
Get those underdog love stories
Up out of your mind.
Stop setting yourself up for failure.
Think realistically! Don't be so blind!
If you're lucky at all there's a chance he may
Invite you into his bed
But afterwards, expect nothing beyond that.
Kill those fantasies in your head.

written in Los Angeles

do you ever hate how perfect someone is?

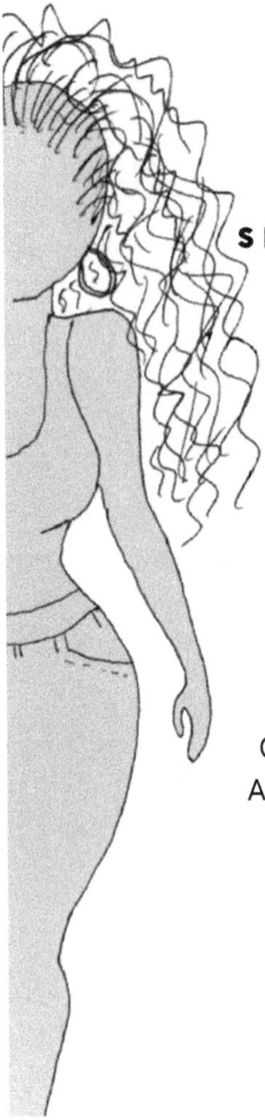

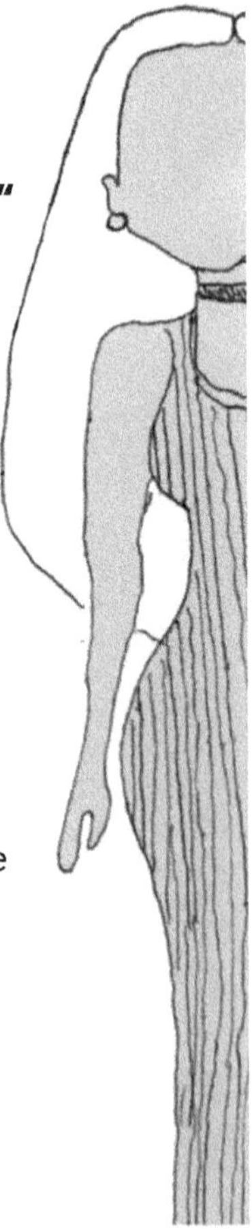

YEAH, SHE'S "BEAUTIFUL"

She's got the skin tone,
She's got the hair,
She's got that beauty
That makes them bulge
In their underwear.
She's got those eyes,
That drive them wild,
She's got that appeal,
That makes them all smile.
She's everything a guy
Could possibly want in a girl.
And she's standing right there
... ruining my world.

written in New York

SHE'S LUCKY!

She's really lucky
'Cause man he's hot!
What everyone wants
She's already got!
Faithful or not,
He clearly sticks around.
He likes her enough
To be consistently down.
What's it like to have 'em?
A guy that fine?
Who in and out of the bedroom
Will spend his time?
Perhaps I'd know if I looked like her.
They seem to get all the guys.
It seems like so many prefer them
And chase after them like some prize.

written in Los Angeles

when your country's beauty standards don't
match what you see in the mirror.

"HI, I'M "UGLY"

I don't have fair skin,
Nor do I have silky hair.
Or even long enough hair
For you to notice me or even want to care.

I'm not too tall at all,
Yet I'm not short enough
To compliment your dominating ego
& be your diamond in the rough.

My body and features? Slender & boney
Not full & squishy to the touch.
No soft, plump, adorable face
That gives most guys a rush.

Instead I'm stuck with high cheek bones
& endless "model-like" features
Which is more like a polite way of saying
That I look like a male creature.

Exotic? Yes. I most certainly am.
.... but not the popular kind.
Beautiful? Sure. I guess so.
But only to a few selection of minds.

Pretty hair? Ehhh, I'm not sure.
Maybe for my own kind.
But far from beautiful in regards to
The common kind to the common mind.

Sexy? Absolutely.
To get laid is beyond easy.
But anything beyond the physical with me,
Almost no one mutually finds appeasing.

"There's beauty in diversity,"
An expression commonly stated.
Yet the kind of beauty I bring to the table,
Seems consistently underrated.

No matter how much I reinvent myself,
It seems I'll never be,
The kind you'd wanna be loyal to
The "type" that'd have you on your knees.

My elementary years seem never ending,
Particularly gym class.
Cause if pursued or considered at all,
I'm usually always picked last.

Rejection is what I know so well,
The carelessly, blunt type.
And time after time after time again
My tears all alone I wipe.

I've developed overcritical self-hate
& almost never feel okay.
Cause if I were really good enough
How could so many just walk away?

"Love yourself," people like to say,

As if it's easy as I, 2, 3.
But many of us don't know how to,
& look to others for guidance to see.

You may not agree with my views
But these are simply MY thoughts.
Created by countless experiences
That chewed & spat me out to rot.

It seems I can never win at all,
And everyone else gets put above me.
I pay the price for my many flaws,
Hi... my name is Ugly.

written in New York

WHEN IT'S NOT YOU PT. 2

You look in the mirror and curse yourself endless times,
"Why didn't they want you?" you try to realize.
Insecurities and self-hate grow stronger,
You doubt yourself before leaving home a bit longer.
Get slight anxiety when meeting someone new,
Terrified you'll relive what you always go through.
Will snap at any sign, of a repeat-heart-break offender.
And get labeled as "crazy," long before "one who's broken, guarded and tender."
Will make endless comparisons trying to see,
What "the Winner" has over you and how you should be.
Still, you've been conditioned to keep hope 'til you'll find,
That long term validation that'll help ease your suffering mind.
'Til then your experiences will haunt your mind and imbue.
You'll continue to tear yourself to pieces, searching for answers...
When it's not you.

written in Los Angeles

"IF AALIYAH"

I wonder if Aaliyah ever felt insecure.
Or ever thought "Man I wish I looked like her."
I wonder how many times she got shitted on,
Until she finally came across the guy who was that one.
I wonder if she ever looked in the mirror & saw flaws to fix.
Or if instead she'd say to herself, "nah, I got this."
It seems now she gets more love & recognition than she ever did alive.
It's funny how no one cares 'til someone dies.
I wonder if Aaliyah ever got heartbroken & thought,
"Maybe a curvier figure, or a different ethnicity wouldn't get me this crap I've gotten."
Aaliyah, a girl so pretty, with swag so unique.
I wonder if behind the smile, did things ever seem bleak.
How much rejection she encountered & how it'd make her feel.
If she ever thought about calling it quits or just continued living for the thrill.
I wonder how many assholes crossed Aaliyah's path.
How many dehumanized her & saw her as just a piece of ass.
I wonder how many nights she cried alone,
Feeling misunderstood with no shoulder to lean on.
I wonder if still alive how many admirers she'd really have,
Or if she'd be overlooked for the next curvier figure or popular lad.
It's easy to look at someone and see,
Their exterior, their flaws or their beauty.
But what's behind the smile is what's truly,
The mystery that many never care to see.

written in New York

ME...

I'm kinda smooth,
Kinda not,
Kinda awkward,
Kinda hot,
Kinda shy,
Yet outspoken,
A good girl, yes,
& naughty when awoken.
Kinda optimistic,
Kinda hurt & bitter,
Determined to win,
But sometimes a quitter.
Confident at times,
But mostly insecure,
Proud to be me,
But wish I were her.
Plenty of wasted time,
Yet here I am still
Awaiting that confirmation,
That this is all worthwhile.

written in Los Angeles

PARTY OVER

...FOR NOW

ABOUT THE AUTHOR

Born and raised the daughter of a minister in Cincinnati, Ohio, Joslyn Kyler-Victoria O'Neal graduated with a Bachelor of Arts from Xavier University. Not long after finishing school, she relocated to NYC to expand her horizons and pursue self-fulfilling endeavors. After a five-year residency in NYC, Kyler relocated to Los Angeles, California where she currently involves herself in various creative platforms from singing and song writing, to poetry, dance and acting.

www.kyleroneal.com

CPSIA information can be obtained
at www.ICGtesting.com
Printed in the USA
FSHW010606211019
63212FS

9 780578 570150